MznLnx

Missing Links Exam Preps

Exam Prep for

Strategic Management in Action

Coulter, 3rd Edition

The MznLnx Exam Prep is your link from the texbook and lecture to your exams.
The MznLnx Exam Preps are unauthorized and comprehensive reviews of your textbooks.

All material provided by MznLnx and Rico Publications (c) 2010
Textbook publishers and textbook authors do not particpate in or contribute to these reviews.

MznLnx

Rico Publications

Exam Prep for Strategic Management in Action
3rd Edition
Coulter

Publisher: Raymond Houge
Assistant Editor: Michael Rouger
Text and Cover Designer: Lisa Buckner
Marketing Manager: Sara Swagger
Project Manager, Editorial Production: Jerry Emerson
Art Director: Vernon Lowerui

Product Manager: Dave Mason
Editorial Assitant: Rachel Guzmanji
Pedagogy: Debra Long
Cover Image: Jim Reed/Getty Images
Text and Cover Printer: City Printing, Inc.
Compositor: Media Mix, Inc.

(c) 2010 Rico Publications

ALL RIGHTS RESERVED. No part of this work covered by the copyright may be reproduced or used in any form or by an means--graphic, electronic, or mechanical, including photocopying, recording, taping, Web distribution, information storage, and retrieval systems, or in any other manner--without the written permission of the publisher.

Printed in the United States
ISBN:

For more information about our products, contact us at:
Dave.Mason@RicoPublications.com

For permission to use material from this text or product, submit a request online to:
Dave.Mason@RicoPublications.com

Contents

CHAPTER 1
Introducing the concepts — 1

CHAPTER 2
The context of managing strategically — 6

CHAPTER 3
Assessing opportunities and threats : doing an external analysis — 11

CHAPTER 4
Assessing strengths and weaknesses : doing an internal analysis — 22

CHAPTER 5
Functional strategies — 25

CHAPTER 6
Competitive strategies — 39

CHAPTER 7
Corporate strategies — 42

CHAPTER 8
Strategic management in other organization types — 48

ANSWER KEY — 51

TO THE STUDENT

COMPREHENSIVE

The *MznLnx* Exam Prep series is designed to help you pass your exams. Editors at MznLnx review your textbooks and then prepare these practice exams to help you master the textbook material. Unlike study guides, workbooks, and practice tests provided by the texkbook publisher and textbook authors, *MznLnx* gives you **all** of the material in each chapter in exam form, not just samples, so you can be sure to nail your exam.

MECHANICAL

The MznLnx Exam Prep series creates exams that will help you learn the subject matter as well as test you on your understanding. Each question is designed to help you master the concept. Just working through the exams, you gain an understanding of the subject--its a simple mechanical process that produces success.

INTEGRATED STUDY GUIDE AND REVIEW

MznLnx is not just a set of exams designed to test you, its also a comprehensive review of the subject content. Each exam question is also a review of the concept, making sure that you will get the answer correct without having to go to other sources of material. You learn as you go! Its the easiest way to pass an exam.

HUMOR

Studying can be tedious and dry. MznLnx's instructional design includes moderate humor within the exam questions on occassion, to break the tedium and revitalize the brain

Chapter 1. Introducing the concepts

1. _____, widely known as F. W. Taylor, was an American mechanical engineer who sought to improve industrial efficiency. He is regarded as the father of scientific management, and was one of the first management consultants.

Taylor was one of the intellectual leaders of the Efficiency Movement and his ideas, broadly conceived, were highly influential in the Progressive Era.

   a. Douglas N. Daft
   b. Geoffrey Colvin
   c. Frederick Winslow Taylor
   d. Jonah Jacob Goldberg

2. _____ refers to metrics and measures of output from production processes, per unit of input. Labor _____, for example, is typically measured as a ratio of output per labor-hour, an input. _____ may be conceived of as a metrics of the technical or engineering efficiency of production.
   a. Master production schedule
   b. Remanufacturing
   c. Productivity
   d. Value engineering

3. Procter is a surname, and may also refer to:

- Bryan Waller Procter (pseud. Barry Cornwall), English poet
- Goodwin Procter, American law firm
- _____, consumer products multinational

   a. Downstream
   b. Master and Servant Acts
   c. Strict liability
   d. Procter ' Gamble

4. _____ is a concept in ethics with several meanings. It is often used synonymously with such concepts as responsibility, answerability, enforcement, blameworthiness, liability and other terms associated with the expectation of account-giving. As an aspect of governance, it has been central to discussions related to problems in both the public and private (corporation) worlds.
   a. Usury
   b. A Stake in the Outcome
   c. A4e
   d. Accountability

Chapter 1. Introducing the concepts

5. A _____ is a body of elected or appointed members who jointly oversee the activities of a company or organization. The body sometimes has a different name, such as board of trustees, board of governors, board of managers, or executive board. It is often simply referred to as 'the board.'

A board's activities are determined by the powers, duties, and responsibilities delegated to it or conferred on it by an authority outside itself.

   a. Board of directors
   b. Competition law
   c. Foreign Corrupt Practices Act
   d. Clean Water Act

6. A chief executive officer (_____) or chief executive is one of the highest-ranking corporate officer (executive) or administrator in charge of total management. An individual selected as President and _____ of a corporation, company, organization, or agency, reports to the board of directors. In internal communication and press releases, many companies capitalize the term and those of other high positions, even when they are not proper nouns.
   a. Director of communications
   b. Chief executive officer
   c. Portfolio manager
   d. CEO

7. A _____ or chief executive is one of the highest-ranking corporate officer (executive) or administrator in charge of total management. An individual selected as President and _____ of a corporation, company, organization, or agency, reports to the board of directors. In internal communication and press releases, many companies capitalize the term and those of other high positions, even when they are not proper nouns.
   a. Chief brand officer
   b. Financial analyst
   c. Purchasing manager
   d. Chief executive officer

8. While _____ literally refers to a person responsible for the performance of duties involved in running an organization, the exact meaning of the role is variable, depending on the organization.

While there is no clear line between executive or principal and inferior officers, principal officers are high-level officials in the executive branch of U.S. government such as department heads of independent agencies. In Humphrey's Executor v. United States, 295 U.S. 602 (1935), the Court distinguished between _____s and quasi-legislative or quasi-judicial officers by stating that the former serve at the pleasure of the President and may be removed at his discretion.

a. Australian Fair Pay and Conditions Standard
b. Executive officer
c. Unreported employment
d. Easement

9. _____ in its literal sense is the process of transformation of local or regional phenomena into global ones. It can be described as a process by which the people of the world are unified into a single society and function together.

This process is a combination of economic, technological, sociocultural and political forces.

a. Globalization
b. Collaborative Planning, Forecasting and Replenishment
c. Histogram
d. Cost Management

10. The _____ is an international organization designed by its founders to supervise and liberalize international trade. The organization officially commenced on 1 January 1995, under the Marrakesh Agreement, succeeding the 1947 General Agreement on Tariffs and Trade (GATT.)

The _____ deals with regulation of trade between participating countries; it provides a framework for negotiating and formalising trade agreements, and a dispute resolution process aimed at enforcing participants' adherence to _____ agreements which are signed by representatives of member governments and ratified by their parliaments.

a. Network planning and design
b. 1990 Clean Air Act
c. National Institute for Occupational Safety and Health
d. World Trade Organization

11. _____ is the set of processes, customs, policies, laws, and institutions affecting the way a corporation (or company) is directed, administered or controlled. _____ also includes the relationships among the many stakeholders involved and the goals for which the corporation is governed. The principal stakeholders are the shareholders/members, management, and the board of directors.
a. Guarantee
b. Corporate governance
c. Flextime
d. No-FEAR Act

Chapter 1. Introducing the concepts

12. The _____ of 2002 (Pub.L. 107-204, 116 Stat. 745, enacted July 30, 2002), also known as the Public Company Accounting Reform and Investor Protection Act of 2002 and commonly called Sarbanes-Oxley, Sarbox or SOX, is a United States federal law enacted on July 30, 2002, as a reaction to a number of major corporate and accounting scandals including those affecting Enron, Tyco International, Adelphia, Peregrine Systems and WorldCom.
    a. Sarbanes-Oxley Act of 2002
    b. Fair Labor Standards Act
    c. Letter of credit
    d. Sarbanes-Oxley Act

13. _____, commonly known as e-commerce, consists of the buying and selling of products or services over electronic systems such as the Internet and other computer networks. The amount of trade conducted electronically has grown extraordinarily with widespread Internet usage. The use of commerce is conducted in this way, spurring and drawing on innovations in electronic funds transfer, supply chain management, Internet marketing, online transaction processing, electronic data interchange (EDI), inventory management systems, and automated data collection systems.
    a. A4e
    b. Online shopping
    c. A Stake in the Outcome
    d. Electronic Commerce

14. _____, commonly referred to as 'eBusiness' or 'e-Business', may be defined as the utilization of information and communication technologies (ICT) in support of all the activities of business. Commerce constitutes the exchange of products and services between businesses, groups and individuals and hence can be seen as one of the essential activities of any business. Hence, electronic commerce or eCommerce focuses on the use of ICT to enable the external activities and relationships of the business with individuals, groups and other businesses.
    a. A Stake in the Outcome
    b. A4e
    c. AAAI
    d. Electronic business

15. An _____ is a private computer network that uses Internet technologies to securely share any part of an organization's information or operational systems with its employees. Sometimes the term refers only to the organization's internal website, but often it is a more extensive part of the organization's computer infrastructure and private websites are an important component and focal point of internal communication and collaboration.

An _____ is built from the same concepts and technologies used for the Internet, such as client-server computing and the Internet Protocol Suite (TCP/IP.)

a. A4e
b. A Stake in the Outcome
c. Intranet
d. AAAI

16. A _____ is a framework for creating economic, social, and/or other forms of value. The term _____ is thus used for a broad range of informal and formal descriptions to represent core aspects of a business, including purpose, offerings, strategies, infrastructure, organizational structures, trading practices, and operational processes and policies.

Conceptualizations of _____s try to formalize informal descriptions into building blocks and their relationships.

a. Gap analysis
b. Business networking
c. Business model design
d. Business model

17. A _____ is a name or trademark connected with a product or producer. _____s have become increasingly important components of culture and the economy, now being described as 'cultural accessories and personal philosophies'.

Some people distinguish the psychological aspect of a _____ from the experiential aspect.

a. Brand
b. Brand extension
c. Brand loyalty
d. Brand awareness

Chapter 2. The context of managing strategically

1. _____ is one of the four elements of marketing mix. An organization or set of organizations (go-betweens) involved in the process of making a product or service available for use or consumption by a consumer or business user.

The other three parts of the marketing mix are product, pricing, and promotion.

   a. Matching theory
   b. Job creation programs
   c. Distribution
   d. Missing completely at random

2. _____ is, in very basic words, a position a firm occupies against its competitors.

According to Michael Porter, the three methods for creating a sustainable _____ are through:

1. Cost leadership

2. Differentiation

3. Focus (economics)

   a. Competitive advantage
   b. Theory Z
   c. 28-hour day
   d. 1990 Clean Air Act

3. _____ is an area of knowledge within organizational theory that studies models and theories about the way an organization learns and adapts.

In Organizational development (OD), learning is a characteristic of an adaptive organization, i.e., an organization that is able to sense changes in signals from its environment (both internal and external) and adapt accordingly.

   a. AAAI
   b. Organizational learning
   c. A4e
   d. A Stake in the Outcome

Chapter 2. The context of managing strategically

4. The _____ is an economic tool used to determine the strategic resources available to a firm. The fundamental principle of the _____ is that the basis for a competitive advantage of a firm lies primarily in the application of the bundle of valuable resources at the firm's disposal (Wernerfelt, 1984, p172; Rumelt, 1984, p557-558.) To transform a short-run competitive advantage into a sustained competitive advantage requires that these resources are heterogeneous in nature and not perfectly mobile (Barney, 1991, p105-106; Peteraf, 1993, p180).
   a. Catfish effect
   b. Resource-based view
   c. Frenemy
   d. Business philosophy

5. _____ is an increasingly broadening term with which an organization, or other human system describes the combination of traditionally administrative personnel functions with acquisition and application of skills, knowledge and experience, Employee Relations and resource planning at various levels. The field draws upon concepts developed in Industrial/Organizational Psychology and System Theory. _____ has at least two related interpretations depending on context. The original usage derives from political economy and economics, where it was traditionally called labor, one of four factors of production although this perspective is changing as a function of new and ongoing research into more strategic approaches at national levels. This first usage is used more in terms of '_____ development', and can go beyond just organizations to the level of nations. The more traditional usage within corporations and businesses refers to the individuals within a firm or agency, and to the portion of the organization that deals with hiring, firing, training, and other personnel issues, typically referred to as `_____ management'.
   a. Human resources
   b. Progressive discipline
   c. Human resource management
   d. Bradford Factor

6. _____ is a business Advocate term for an element which is necessary for an organization or project to achieve its mission. They are the critical factors or activities required for ensuring the success of your business. The term was initially used in the world of data analysis, and business analysis.
   a. Collaborative leadership
   b. Customer satisfaction
   c. Critical success factor
   d. Business hours

7. A _____ is a set of exclusive rights granted by a state to an inventor or his assignee for a limited period of time in exchange for a disclosure of an invention.

The procedure for granting _____s, the requirements placed on the _____ee and the extent of the exclusive rights vary widely between countries according to national laws and international agreements. Typically, however, a _____ application must include one or more claims defining the invention which must be new, inventive, and useful or industrially applicable.

a. Federal Trade Commission Act
b. Food, Drug, and Cosmetic Act
c. Labor Management Reporting and Disclosure Act
d. Patent

8. The term '_____' refers to the concept of collecting information and attempting to spot a pattern in the information. In some fields of study, the term '_____' has more formally-defined meanings.

In project management _____ is a mathematical technique that uses historical results to predict future outcome.

a. Stepwise regression
b. Least squares
c. Trend analysis
d. Regression analysis

9. _____ in its literal sense is the process of transformation of local or regional phenomena into global ones. It can be described as a process by which the people of the world are unified into a single society and function together.

This process is a combination of economic, technological, sociocultural and political forces.

a. Cost Management
b. Histogram
c. Collaborative Planning, Forecasting and Replenishment
d. Globalization

10. _____ is subcontracting a process, such as product design or manufacturing, to a third-party company. The decision to outsource is often made in the interest of lowering cost or making better use of time and energy costs, redirecting or conserving energy directed at the competencies of a particular business, or to make more efficient use of land, labor, capital, (information) technology and resources. _____ became part of the business lexicon during the 1980s.

a. Outsourcing
b. Unemployment insurance
c. Opinion leadership
d. Operant conditioning

11. _____ refers to metrics and measures of output from production processes, per unit of input. Labor _____, for example, is typically measured as a ratio of output per labor-hour, an input. _____ may be conceived of as a metrics of the technical or engineering efficiency of production.

a. Remanufacturing
b. Productivity
c. Master production schedule
d. Value engineering

12. _____ is a form of corporate self-regulation integrated into a business model. Ideally, _____ policy would function as a built-in, self-regulating mechanism whereby business would monitor and ensure their adherence to law, ethical standards, and international norms. Business would embrace responsibility for the impact of their activities on the environment, consumers, employees, communities, stakeholders and all other members of the public sphere.
    a. 28-hour day
    b. Corporate social responsibility
    c. 33 Strategies of War
    d. 1990 Clean Air Act

13. Procter is a surname, and may also refer to:

    - Bryan Waller Procter (pseud. Barry Cornwall), English poet
    - Goodwin Procter, American law firm
    - _____, consumer products multinational

    a. Downstream
    b. Master and Servant Acts
    c. Procter ' Gamble
    d. Strict liability

14. A _____ is the term given to a company that facilitates the learning of its members and continuously transforms itself. _____s develop as a result of the pressures facing modern organizations and enables them to remain competitive in the business environment. A _____ has five main features; systems thinking, personal mastery, mental models, shared vision and team learning.
    a. Hoshin Kanri
    b. 1990 Clean Air Act
    c. Quality function deployment
    d. Learning organization

15. The concept of a _____ refers to the process of social learning that occurs and shared sociocultural practices that emerge and evolve when people who have common goals interact as they strive towards those goals.

The term was founded on the work of a few cognitive anthropologists, namely Barbara Rogoff (1985) and Jean Lave, who attempted to explain and describe learning that occurs in apprenticeship situations. Later, Lave, in collaboration with Etienne Wenger (1991) originated the construct legitimate peripheral participation in their studies of five apprenticeship situations: midwives in the Yucatan, Vai and Gola tailors, naval quartermasters, meat cutters, and a group of alcoholics anonymous.

   a. 28-hour day
   b. Community of practice
   c. 1990 Clean Air Act
   d. 33 Strategies of War

Chapter 3. Assessing opportunities and threats : doing an external analysis

1. _____ is an interdisciplinary field of science and the study of the nature of complex systems in nature, society, and science. More specifically, it is a framework by which one can analyze and/or describe any group of objects that work in concert to produce some result. This could be a single organism, any organization or society, or any electro-mechanical or informational artifact.
   a. 28-hour day
   b. Systems theory
   c. Systems thinking
   d. 1990 Clean Air Act

2. _____ is a process of gathering, analyzing, and dispensing information for tactical or strategic purposes. The _____ process entails obtaining both factual and subjective information on the business environments in which a company is operating or considering entering.

There are three ways of scanning the business environment:

- Ad-hoc scanning - Short term, infrequent examinations usually initiated by a crisis
- Regular scanning - Studies done on a regular schedule (say, once a year)
- Continuous scanning(also called continuous learning) - continuous structured data collection and processing on a broad range of environmental factors

Most commentators feel that in today's turbulent business environment the best scanning method available is continuous scanning. This allows the firm to :

-act quickly-take advantage of opportunities before competitors do-respond to environmental threats before significant damage is done

   a. Environmental scanning
   b. A Stake in the Outcome
   c. AAAI
   d. A4e

3. In economics, _____ are obstacles in the path of a firm which wants to leave a given market or industrial sector. These obstacles often cost the firm financially to leave the market and may prohibit it doing so.

If the barriers of exit are significant; a firm may be forced to continue competing in a market, as the costs of leaving may be higher than those incurred if they continue competing in the market.

Chapter 3. Assessing opportunities and threats : doing an external analysis

   a. 28-hour day
   b. 1990 Clean Air Act
   c. 33 Strategies of War
   d. Barriers to exit

4. A _____ or transnational corporation is a corporation or enterprise that manages production or delivers services in more than one country. It can also be referred to as an international corporation.

The first modern _____ is generally thought to be the Dutch East India Company, established in 1602.

   a. Command center
   b. Financial Accounting Standards Board
   c. Multinational corporation
   d. Small and medium enterprises

5. In economics and especially in the theory of competition, _____ are obstacles in the path of a firm that make it difficult to enter a given market.

_____ are the source of a firm's pricing power - the ability of a firm to raise prices without losing all its customers.

The term refers to hindrances that an individual may face while trying to gain entrance into a profession or trade.

   a. Predatory pricing
   b. Barriers to entry
   c. 28-hour day
   d. 1990 Clean Air Act

6. _____, in microeconomics, are the cost advantages that a business obtains due to expansion. They are factors that cause a producer's average cost per unit to fall as scale is increased. _____ is a long run concept and refers to reductions in unit cost as the size of a facility, or scale, increases.
   a. Economies of scope
   b. Economies of scale
   c. A Stake in the Outcome
   d. A4e

Chapter 3. Assessing opportunities and threats : doing an external analysis

7. Network externalities resemble economies of scale, but they are not considered such because they are a function of the number of users of a good or service in an industry, not of the production efficiency within a business. _____ are only considered examples of network externalities if they are driven by demand side economies.

Formally, a production function $f(K,L)$ is defined to have:

- constant returns to scale if (for any constant a greater than or equal to 0) $f(aK, aL) = af(K,L)$
- increasing returns to scale if (for any constant a greater than 1) $f(aK, aL) > af(K,L)$
- decreasing returns to scale if (for any constant a greater than 1) $f(aK, aL) < af(K,L)$

where K and L are factors of production, capital and labour, respectively.

As an example, the Cobb-Douglas functional form has constant returns to scale when the sum of the exponents adds up to one.

a. AAAI
b. A4e
c. Economies of scale external to the firm
d. A Stake in the Outcome

8. A _____ is a business that is privately owned and operated, with a small number of employees and relatively low volume of sales. The legal definition of 'small' often varies by country and industry, but is generally under 100 employees in the United States and under 50 employees in the European Union. In comparison, the definition of mid-sized business by the number of employees is generally under 500 in the U.S. and 250 for the European Union.

a. Critical Success Factor
b. Small business
c. Pre-determined overhead rate
d. Golden Boot Compensation

9. An _____ is a person who has possession of an enterprise and assumes significant accountability for the inherent risks and the outcome. It is an ambitious leader who combines land, labor, and capital to create and market new goods or services. The term is a loanword from French and was first defined by the Irish economist Richard Cantillon.

a. A Stake in the Outcome
b. A4e
c. AAAI
d. Entrepreneur

14 *Chapter 3. Assessing opportunities and threats : doing an external analysis*

10. The _____ is a bank regulation, which sets a framework on how banks and depository institutions must handle their capital. The categorization of assets and capital is highly standardized so that it can be risk weighted. Internationally, the Basel Committee on Banking Supervision housed at the Bank for International Settlements influence each country's banking _____s.

   a. Lock box
   b. 1990 Clean Air Act
   c. Reserve requirement
   d. Capital requirement

11. In marketing, _____ is the process of distinguishing the differences of a product or offering from others, to make it more attractive to a particular target market. This involves differentiating it from competitors' products as well as one's own product offerings.

   a. PEST analysis
   b. Market share
   c. Market development
   d. Product differentiation

12. _____ is a concept related to the relative abilities of parties in a situation to exert influence over each other. If both parties are on an equal footing in a debate, then they will have equal _____, such as in a perfectly competitive market, or between an evenly matched monopoly and monopsony.

   There are a number of fields where the concept of _____ has proven crucial to coherent analysis: game theory, labour economics, collective bargaining arrangements, diplomatic negotiations, settlement of litigation, the price of insurance, and any negotiation in general.

   a. Trade credit
   b. 1990 Clean Air Act
   c. Buy-sell agreement
   d. Bargaining power

13. _____ is one of the four elements of marketing mix. An organization or set of organizations (go-betweens) involved in the process of making a product or service available for use or consumption by a consumer or business user.

   The other three parts of the marketing mix are product, pricing, and promotion.

Chapter 3. Assessing opportunities and threats : doing an external analysis

a. Distribution
b. Job creation programs
c. Missing completely at random
d. Matching theory

14. Switching barriers or _____s are terms used in microeconomics, strategic management, and marketing to describe any impediment to a customer's changing of suppliers.

In many markets, consumers are forced to incur costs when switching from one supplier to another. These costs are called _____s and can come in many different shapes.

a. Corporate strategy
b. Strategic business unit
c. Strategic group
d. Switching cost

15. In economics, business, retail, and accounting, a _____ is the value of money that has been used up to produce something, and hence is not available for use anymore. In economics, a _____ is an alternative that is given up as a result of a decision. In business, the _____ may be one of acquisition, in which case the amount of money expended to acquire it is counted as _____.

a. Fixed costs
b. Cost overrun
c. Cost
d. Cost allocation

16. _____ or _____ data refers to selected population characteristics as used in government, marketing or opinion research, or the _____ profiles used in such research. Note the distinction from the term 'demography' Commonly-used _____s include race, age, income, disabilities, mobility (in terms of travel time to work or number of vehicles available), educational attainment, home ownership, employment status, and even location.

a. Adam Smith
b. Abraham Harold Maslow
c. Affiliation
d. Demographic

17. _____, commonly abbreviated to Gen X, is a term used to refer to a generational cohort of children born after the baby boom ended and usually prior to the 1980s

Chapter 3. Assessing opportunities and threats : doing an external analysis

The term _____ has been used in demography, the social sciences, and marketing, though it is most often used in popular culture.

In the U.S. _____ was originally referred to as the 'baby bust' generation because of the drop in the birth rate following the baby boom.

   a. Generation X
   b. Affiliation
   c. Abraham Harold Maslow
   d. Adam Smith

18. _____ is a cross-disciplinary area concerned with protecting the safety, health and welfare of people engaged in work or employment. The goal of all _____ programs is to foster a work free safe environment. As a secondary effect, it may also protect co-workers, family members, employers, customers, suppliers, nearby communities, and other members of the public who are impacted by the workplace environment.
   a. A Stake in the Outcome
   b. A4e
   c. AAAI
   d. Occupational Safety and Health

19. The United States _____ is an agency of the United States Department of Labor. It was created by Congress under the Occupational Safety and Health Act, signed by President Richard M. Nixon, on December 29, 1970. Its mission is to prevent work-related injuries, illnesses, and deaths by issuing and enforcing rules (called standards) for workplace safety and health.
   a. Unemployment insurance
   b. Opinion leadership
   c. Operant conditioning
   d. Occupational Safety and Health Administration

20. The _____ of 1990 (ADA) is the short title of United States (Pub.L. 101-336, 104 Stat. 327, enacted July 26, 1990), codified at 42 U.S.C. § 12101 et seq. It was signed into law on July 26, 1990, by President George H. W. Bush, and later amended with changes effective January 1, 2009. The ADA is a wide-ranging civil rights law that prohibits, under certain circumstances, discrimination based on disability. It affords similar protections against discrimination to Americans with disabilities as the Civil Rights Act of 1964,

a. Australian labour law
b. Equal Pay Act of 1963
c. Americans with Disabilities Act
d. Employment discrimination

21. The _____ is a United States statute that was passed in response to a series of United States Supreme Court decisions which limited the rights of employees who had sued their employers for discrimination. The Act represented the first effort since the passage of the Civil Rights Act of 1964 to modify some of the basic procedural and substantive rights provided by federal law in employment discrimination cases. It provided for the right to trial by jury on discrimination claims and introduced the possibility of emotional distress damages, while limiting the amount that a jury could award

The 1991 Act combined elements from two different civil rights acts of the past: the Civil Rights Act of 1866, better known by the number assigned to it in the codification of federal laws as 'Section 1981', and the employment-related provisions of the Civil Rights Act of 1964, generally referred to as 'Title VII', its location within the Act.

a. Covenant
b. Negligence in employment
c. Civil Rights Act of 1991
d. Resource Conservation and Recovery Act

22. _____ is a broad label that refers to any individuals or households that use goods and services generated within the economy. The concept of a _____ is used in different contexts, so that the usage and significance of the term may vary.

Typically when business people and economists talk of _____s they are talking about person as _____, an aggregated commodity item with little individuality other than that expressed in the buy/not-buy decision.

a. 33 Strategies of War
b. 1990 Clean Air Act
c. 28-hour day
d. Consumer

23. The _____ was enacted in 1972 by the United States Congress. It established the United States Consumer Product Safety Commission as an independent agency of the United States federal government and defined its basic authority. The act gives CPSC the power to develop safety standards and pursue recalls for products that present unreasonable or substantial risks of injury or death to consumers.

Chapter 3. Assessing opportunities and threats : doing an external analysis

a. 1990 Clean Air Act
b. 33 Strategies of War
c. Consumer Product Safety Act
d. 28-hour day

24. The _____ of 1996 (18 U.S.C. § 1831-1839) makes the theft or misappropriation of a trade secret a federal crime. Unlike Espionage, which is governed by Title 18 U.S. Code Sections 792 - 799, the offense involves commercial information, not classified or national defense information.
a. A Stake in the Outcome
b. Economic Espionage Act
c. A4e
d. AAAI

25. _____ is a contract between two parties, one being the employer and the other being the employee. An employee may be defined as: 'A person in the service of another under any contract of hire, express or implied, oral or written, where the employer has the power or right to control and direct the employee in the material details of how the work is to be performed.' Black's Law Dictionary page 471 (5th ed. 1979.)
a. Employment rate
b. Exit interview
c. Employment
d. Employment counsellor

26. The term _____ was created by President Lyndon B. Johnson when he signed Executive Order 11246 on September 24, 1965, created to prohibit federal contractors from discriminating against employees on the basis of race, sex, creed, religion, color, or national origin. In more recent times, most employers have also added sexual orientation to the list of non-discrimination.

The Executive Order also required contractors to implement affirmative action plans to increase the participation of minorities and women in the workplace.

a. A Stake in the Outcome
b. A4e
c. AAAI
d. Equal Employment Opportunity

Chapter 3. Assessing opportunities and threats : doing an external analysis

27. The _____ is a United States labor law allowing an employee to take unpaid leave due to a serious health condition that makes the employee unable to perform his job or to care for a sick family member or to care for a new son or daughter (including by birth, adoption or foster care.) The bill was among the first signed into law by President Bill Clinton in his first term.

   a. Family and Medical Leave Act of 1993
   b. Sarbanes-Oxley Act of 2002
   c. Contributory negligence
   d. Harvester Judgment

28. The _____ is a trilateral trade bloc in North America created by the governments of the United States, Canada, and Mexico. The agreement creating the trade bloc came into force on January 1, 1994. It superseded the Canada-United States Free Trade Agreement between the U.S. and Canada.

   a. Career portfolios
   b. North American Free Trade Agreement
   c. Business war game
   d. Trade union

29. The _____ is the primary federal law which governs occupational health and safety in the private sector and federal government in the United States. It was enacted by Congress in 1970 and was signed by President Richard Nixon on December 29, 1970. Its main goal is to ensure that employers provide employees with an environment free from recognized hazards, such as exposure to toxic chemicals, excessive noise levels, mechanical dangers, heat or cold stress, or unsanitary conditions.

   a. United States Department of Justice
   b. Unemployment and Farm Relief Act
   c. Occupational Safety and Health Act
   d. Unemployment Action Center

30. _____ is the process of learning a new skill or trade, often in response to a change in the economic environment. Generally it reflects changes in profession choice rather than an 'upward' movement in the same field.

   There is some controversy surrounding the use of _____ to offset economic changes caused by free trade and automation.

   a. Suspension training
   b. Krauthammer
   c. Compliance Training
   d. Retraining

Chapter 3. Assessing opportunities and threats : doing an external analysis

31. The _____ of 2002 (Pub.L. 107-204, 116 Stat. 745, enacted July 30, 2002), also known as the Public Company Accounting Reform and Investor Protection Act of 2002 and commonly called Sarbanes-Oxley, Sarbox or SOX, is a United States federal law enacted on July 30, 2002, as a reaction to a number of major corporate and accounting scandals including those affecting Enron, Tyco International, Adelphia, Peregrine Systems and WorldCom.
   a. Sarbanes-Oxley Act
   b. Sarbanes-Oxley Act of 2002
   c. Letter of credit
   d. Fair Labor Standards Act

32. The _____ is a United States labor law which protects employees, their families, and communities by requiring most employers with 100 or more employees to provide sixty- (60) calendar-day advance notification of plant closings and mass layoffs of employees. It was enacted in 1989.

   Employees entitled to notice under the _____ include managers and supervisors, hourly wage, and salaried workers.

   a. Robinson-Patman Act
   b. Leave of absence
   c. Worker Adjustment and Retraining Notification Act
   d. Non-disclosure agreement

33. A _____ is a form of qualitative research in which a group of people are asked about their attitude towards a product, service, concept, advertisement, idea, or packaging. Questions are asked in an interactive group setting where participants are free to talk with other group members.

   The first _____s were created at the Bureau of Applied Social Research by associate director, sociologist Robert K. Merton.

   a. Market analysis
   b. Focus group
   c. 1990 Clean Air Act
   d. Marketing research

34. The term '_____' refers to the concept of collecting information and attempting to spot a pattern in the information. In some fields of study, the term '_____' has more formally-defined meanings.

   In project management _____ is a mathematical technique that uses historical results to predict future outcome.

a. Least squares
b. Stepwise regression
c. Trend analysis
d. Regression analysis

35. _____ is the original form of externally-oriented business intelligence that preceded Knowledge Management or Data Mining as the primary concern of executives responsible for increasing market share.
a. Competitor or Competitive Intelligence
b. 28-hour day
c. Competitor analysis
d. 1990 Clean Air Act

Chapter 4. Assessing strengths and weaknesses : doing an internal analysis

1. _____ is an increasingly broadening term with which an organization, or other human system describes the combination of traditionally administrative personnel functions with acquisition and application of skills, knowledge and experience, Employee Relations and resource planning at various levels. The field draws upon concepts developed in Industrial/Organizational Psychology and System Theory. _____ has at least two related interpretations depending on context. The original usage derives from political economy and economics, where it was traditionally called labor, one of four factors of production although this perspective is changing as a function of new and ongoing research into more strategic approaches at national levels. This first usage is used more in terms of '_____ development', and can go beyond just organizations to the level of nations . The more traditional usage within corporations and businesses refers to the individuals within a firm or agency, and to the portion of the organization that deals with hiring, firing, training, and other personnel issues, typically referred to as `_____ management'.
   a. Progressive discipline
   b. Bradford Factor
   c. Human resource management
   d. Human resources

2. _____ is something that a firm can do well and that meets the following three conditions:

Competencies are things that companys execute well across several business units or product sectors.

Firms usually have few competencies, but these are usually less liable to change rapidly.

   1. It provides consumer benefits
   2. It is not easy for competitors to imitate
   3. It can be leveraged widely to many products and markets.

A _____ can take various forms, including technical/subject matter know-how, a reliable process and/or close relationships with customers and suppliers (Mascarenhas et al. 1998.)

   a. Learning-by-doing
   b. Core competency
   c. NAIRU
   d. Dominant Design

3. The _____ is a concept from business management that was first described and popularized by Michael Porter in his 1985 best-seller, Competitive Advantage: Creating and Sustaining Superior Performance.

A _____ is a chain of activities. Products pass through all activities of the chain in order and at each activity the product gains some value. The chain of activities gives the products more added value than the sum of added values of all activities. It is important not to mix the concept of the _____ with the costs occurring throughout the activities.

Chapter 4. Assessing strengths and weaknesses : doing an internal analysis

a. Customer relationship management
b. Mass marketing
c. Value chain
d. Market development

4. The general definition of an _____ is an evaluation of a person, organization, system, process, project or product. _____s are performed to ascertain the validity and reliability of information; also to provide an assessment of a system's internal control. The goal of an _____ is to express an opinion on the person / organization/system (etc) in question, under evaluation based on work done on a test basis.
   a. Audit committee
   b. Audit
   c. Internal control
   d. A Stake in the Outcome

5. The term '_____' refers to the concept of collecting information and attempting to spot a pattern in the information. In some fields of study, the term '_____' has more formally-defined meanings.

In project management _____ is a mathematical technique that uses historical results to predict future outcome.

   a. Least squares
   b. Stepwise regression
   c. Regression analysis
   d. Trend analysis

6. _____, in strategic management and marketing is, according to Carlton O'Neal, the percentage or proportion of the total available market or market segment that is being serviced by a company. It can be expressed as a company's sales revenue (from that market) divided by the total sales revenue available in that market. It can also be expressed as a company's unit sales volume (in a market) divided by the total volume of units sold in that market.
   a. Market share
   b. Green marketing
   c. Marketing plan
   d. Business-to-business

7. A _____ is a name or trademark connected with a product or producer. _____s have become increasingly important components of culture and the economy, now being described as 'cultural accessories and personal philosophies'.

Some people distinguish the psychological aspect of a _____ from the experiential aspect.

   a. Brand loyalty
   b. Brand extension
   c. Brand awareness
   d. Brand

Chapter 5. Functional strategies

1. The phrase _____, according to the Organization for Economic Co-operation and Development, refers to 'creative work undertaken on a systematic basis in order to increase the stock of knowledge, including knowledge of man, culture and society, and the use of this stock of knowledge to devise new applications [sic]'

New product design and development is more than often a crucial factor in the survival of a company. In an industry that is fast changing, firms must continually revise their design and range of products. This is necessary due to continuous technology change and development as well as other competitors and the changing preference of customers.

   a. 1990 Clean Air Act
   b. Research and development
   c. 33 Strategies of War
   d. 28-hour day

2. _____ is a process used to manage information technology (IT.) Its primary goal is to ensure that IT capacity meets current and future business requirements in a cost-effective manner. One common interpretation of _____ is described in the ITIL framework .
   a. 28-hour day
   b. Capacity management
   c. 1990 Clean Air Act
   d. 33 Strategies of War

3. In economics, _____ is the desire to own something and the ability to pay for it. The term _____ signifies the ability or the willingness to buy a particular commodity at a given point of time.
   a. 1990 Clean Air Act
   b. 28-hour day
   c. 33 Strategies of War
   d. Demand

4. In economics, _____' is the art or science of controlling economic demand to avoid a recession. In natural resources management and environmental policy more generally, it refers to policies to control consumer demand for environmentally sensitive or harmful goods such as water and energy. Within manufacturing firms the term is used to describe the activities of demand forecasting, planning and order fulfillment.
   a. 28-hour day
   b. 1990 Clean Air Act
   c. 33 Strategies of War
   d. Demand management

Chapter 5. Functional strategies

5. In organizational development (OD), _____ is the application of Socio-Technical Systems principles and techniques to the humanization of work.

The aims of _____ to improved job satisfaction, to improved through-put, to improved quality and to reduced employee problems, e.g., grievances, absenteeism.

Under scientific management people would be directed by reason and the problems of industrial unrest would be appropriately (i.e., scientifically) addressed.

   a. Management process
   b. Path-goal theory
   c. Graduate recruitment
   d. Work design

6. A _____ is a commercial building for storage of goods. _____s are used by manufacturers, importers, exporters, wholesalers, transport businesses, customs, etc. They are usually large plain buildings in industrial areas of cities and towns.
   a. 1990 Clean Air Act
   b. 33 Strategies of War
   c. Warehouse
   d. 28-hour day

7. The _____ is a concept from business management that was first described and popularized by Michael Porter in his 1985 best-seller, Competitive Advantage: Creating and Sustaining Superior Performance.

A _____ is a chain of activities. Products pass through all activities of the chain in order and at each activity the product gains some value. The chain of activities gives the products more added value than the sum of added values of all activities. It is important not to mix the concept of the _____ with the costs occurring throughout the activities.

   a. Value chain
   b. Mass marketing
   c. Customer relationship management
   d. Market development

8. _____ is a term used in various branches of engineering and economic development.

Chapter 5. Functional strategies 27

_____ refers to small premises provided, often by local authorities or economic development agencies, to help new businesses to establish themselves. These typically provide not only physical space and utilities, but also administrative services and links to support and finance organisations, as well as peer support among the tenants.

  a. 1990 Clean Air Act
  b. 33 Strategies of War
  c. Workspace
  d. 28-hour day

9. A _____ is a group of people or organizations sharing one or more characteristics that cause them to have similar product and/or service needs. A true _____ meets all of the following criteria: it is distinct from other segments (different segments have different needs), it is homogeneous within the segment (exhibits common needs); it responds similarly to a market stimulus, and it can be reached by a market intervention. The term is also used when consumers with identical product and/or service needs are divided up into groups so they can be charged different amounts.
  a. Customer relationship management
  b. Context analysis
  c. SWOT analysis
  d. Market segment

10. _____ is an integrated communications-based process through which individuals and communities discover that existing and newly-identified needs and wants may be satisfied by the products and services of others.

_____ is defined by the American _____ Association as the activity, set of institutions, and processes for creating, communicating, delivering, and exchanging offerings that have value for customers, clients, partners, and society at large. The term developed from the original meaning which referred literally to going to market, as in shopping, or going to a market to buy or sell goods or services.

  a. Customer relationship management
  b. Marketing
  c. Market development
  d. Disruptive technology

11. _____ is a form of marketing developed from direct response marketing campaigns conducted in the 1970s and 1980s which emphasizes customer retention and satisfaction, rather than a dominant focus on point-of-sale transactions.

_____ differs from other forms of marketing in that it recognizes the long term value to the firm of keeping customers, as opposed to direct or 'Intrusion' marketing, which focuses upon acquisition of new clients by targeting majority demographics based upon prospective client lists.

Chapter 5. Functional strategies

_____ refers to a long-term and mutually beneficial arrangement wherein both the buyer and seller focus on value enhancement with the goal of providing a more satisfying exchange.

a. Guerrilla marketing
b. Relationship marketing
c. 28-hour day
d. 1990 Clean Air Act

12. In marketing, _____ has come to mean the process by which marketers try to create an image or identity in the minds of their target market for its product, brand, or organization. It is the 'relative competitive comparison' their product occupies in a given market as perceived by the target market.

Re-_____ involves changing the identity of a product, relative to the identity of competing products, in the collective minds of the target market.

a. Customer analytics
b. Context analysis
c. PEST analysis
d. Positioning

13. A _____ is a name or trademark connected with a product or producer. _____s have become increasingly important components of culture and the economy, now being described as 'cultural accessories and personal philosophies'.

Some people distinguish the psychological aspect of a _____ from the experiential aspect.

a. Brand extension
b. Brand loyalty
c. Brand awareness
d. Brand

14. The _____ is generally accepted as the use and specification of the 'four P's' describing the strategic position of a product in the marketplace. One version of the _____ originated in 1948 when James Culliton said that a marketing decision should be a result of something similar to a recipe. This version was used in 1953 when Neil Borden, in his American Marketing Association presidential address, took the recipe idea one step further and coined the term 'marketing-mix'.

a. 28-hour day
b. 1990 Clean Air Act
c. 33 Strategies of War
d. Marketing mix

15. _____ is the difference between the cost of a good or service and its selling price. A _____ is added on to the total cost incurred by the producer of a good or service in order to create a profit. The total cost reflects the total amount of both fixed and variable expenses to produce and distribute a product.
   a. Topics
   b. Markup
   c. Premium pricing
   d. Price points

16. In business and engineering, _____ is the term used to describe the complete process of bringing a new product or service to market. There are two parallel paths involved in the _____ process: one involves the idea generation, product design, and detail engineering; the other involves market research and marketing analysis. Companies typically see _____ as the first stage in generating and commercializing new products within the overall strategic process of product life cycle management used to maintain or grow their market share.
   a. 33 Strategies of War
   b. 28-hour day
   c. 1990 Clean Air Act
   d. New product development

17. _____ Management is the succession of strategies used by management as a product goes through its _____. The conditions in which a product is sold changes over time and must be managed as it moves through its succession of stages.

The _____ goes through many phases, involves many professional disciplines, and requires many skills, tools and processes.

   a. Job hunting
   b. Golden handshake
   c. Strategic Alliance
   d. Product life cycle

18. _____, or Value optimized pricing is a business strategy. It sets selling prices on the perceived value to the customer, rather than on the actual cost of the product, the market price, competitors prices, or the historical price.

Chapter 5. Functional strategies

The goal of value-based pricing is to align price with value delivered.

a. Supervisory board
b. Chief legal officer
c. Value based pricing
d. Centralization

19. _____ is one of the four Ps of the marketing mix. The other three aspects are product, promotion, and place. It is also a key variable in microeconomic price allocation theory.
a. Price floor
b. Pricing
c. Transfer pricing
d. Penetration pricing

20. In business and engineering, new _____ is the term used to describe the complete process of bringing a new product or service to market. There are two parallel paths involved in the NProduct development process: one involves the idea generation, product design, and detail engineering; the other involves market research and marketing analysis. Companies typically see new _____ as the first stage in generating and commercializing new products within the overall strategic process of product life cycle management used to maintain or grow their market share.
a. 28-hour day
b. 33 Strategies of War
c. 1990 Clean Air Act
d. Product development

21. _____ is a form of communication that typically attempts to persuade potential customers to purchase or to consume more of a particular brand of product or service. 'While now central to the contemporary global economy and the reproduction of global production networks, it is only quite recently that _____ has been more than a marginal influence on patterns of sales and production. The formation of modern _____ was intimately bound up with the emergence of new forms of monopoly capitalism around the end of the 19th and beginning of the 20th century as one element in corporate strategies to create, organize and where possible control markets, especially for mass produced consumer goods.
a. AAAI
b. A Stake in the Outcome
c. Advertising
d. A4e

Chapter 5. Functional strategies

22. _____ is a sub-discipline and type of marketing. There are two main definitional characteristics which distinguish it from other types of marketing. The first is that it attempts to send its messages directly to consumers, without the use of intervening media.
   a. 1990 Clean Air Act
   b. 28-hour day
   c. Guthy-Renker
   d. Direct marketing

23. _____ is one of the four elements of marketing mix. An organization or set of organizations (go-betweens) involved in the process of making a product or service available for use or consumption by a consumer or business user.

The other three parts of the marketing mix are product, pricing, and promotion.

   a. Matching theory
   b. Distribution
   c. Job creation programs
   d. Missing completely at random

24. _____ is the practice of managing the flow of information between an organization and its publics. _____ gains an organization or individual exposure to their audiences using topics of public interest and news items that do not require direct payment. Because _____ places exposure in credible third-party outlets, it offers a third-party legitimacy that advertising does not have.
   a. Public relations
   b. 28-hour day
   c. Two-way communication
   d. 1990 Clean Air Act

25. _____ is one of the four aspects of promotional mix. (The other three parts of the promotional mix are advertising, personal selling, and publicity/public relations.) Media and non-media marketing communication are employed for a pre-determined, limited time to increase consumer demand, stimulate market demand or improve product availability.
   a. 1990 Clean Air Act
   b. Coupon
   c. Sales promotion
   d. Word of mouth

Chapter 5. Functional strategies

26. _____ is the management of the flow of goods, information and other resources, including energy and people, between the point of origin and the point of consumption in order to meet the requirements of consumers (frequently, and originally, military organizations.) _____ involves the integration of information, transportation, inventory, warehousing, material-handling, and packaging, and occasionally security. _____ is a channel of the supply chain which adds the value of time and place utility.

   a. Third-party logistics
   b. Logistics
   c. 1990 Clean Air Act
   d. 28-hour day

27. _____, in marketing, manufacturing, call centres and management, is the use of flexible computer-aided manufacturing systems to produce custom output. Those systems combine the low unit costs of mass production processes with the flexibility of individual customization.

   '_____' is the new frontier in business competition for both manufacturing and service industries.

   a. 28-hour day
   b. 33 Strategies of War
   c. 1990 Clean Air Act
   d. Mass customization

28. _____ is an approach to quickly answer multi-dimensional analytical queries. _____ is part of the broader category of business intelligence, which also encompasses relational reporting and data mining. The typical applications of _____ are in business reporting for sales, marketing, management reporting, business process management (BPM), budgeting and forecasting, financial reporting and similar areas.

   a. A4e
   b. AAAI
   c. A Stake in the Outcome
   d. Online analytical processing

29. _____ is an increasingly broadening term with which an organization, or other human system describes the combination of traditionally administrative personnel functions with acquisition and application of skills, knowledge and experience, Employee Relations and resource planning at various levels. The field draws upon concepts developed in Industrial/Organizational Psychology and System Theory. _____ has at least two related interpretations depending on context. The original usage derives from political economy and economics, where it was traditionally called labor, one of four factors of production although this perspective is changing as a function of new and ongoing research into more strategic approaches at national levels. This first usage is used more in terms of '_____ development', and can go beyond just organizations to the level of nations . The more traditional usage within corporations and businesses refers to the individuals within a firm or agency, and to the portion of the organization that deals with hiring, firing, training, and other personnel issues, typically referred to as `_____ management'.

a. Bradford Factor
b. Human resource management
c. Progressive discipline
d. Human resources

30. _____ refers to the stock of skills and knowledge embodied in the ability to perform labor so as to produce economic value. It is the skills and knowledge gained by a worker through education and experience. Many early economic theories refer to it simply as labor, one of three factors of production, and consider it to be a fungible resource -- homogeneous and easily interchangeable.
   a. Productivity management
   b. Market structure
   c. Deflation
   d. Human capital

31. _____ is a method by which the job performance of an employee is evaluated _____ is a part of career development.

_____s are regular reviews of employee performance within organizations

Generally, the aims of a _____ are to:

- Give feedback on performance to employees.
- Identify employee training needs.
- Document criteria used to allocate organizational rewards.
- Form a basis for personnel decisions: salary increases, promotions, disciplinary actions, etc.
- Provide the opportunity for organizational diagnosis and development.
- Facilitate communication between employee and administraton
- Validate selection techniques and human resource policies to meet federal Equal Employment Opportunity requirements.

A common approach to assessing performance is to use a numerical or scalar rating system whereby managers are asked to score an individual against a number of objectives/attributes. In some companies, employees receive assessments from their manager, peers, subordinates and customers while also performing a self assessment.

   a. Human resource management
   b. Personnel management
   c. Progressive discipline
   d. Performance appraisal

Chapter 5. Functional strategies

32. The field of _____ looks at the relationship between management and workers, particularly groups of workers represented by a union.

_____ is an important factor in analyzing 'varieties of capitalism', such as neocorporatism, social democracy, and neoliberalism

   a. Overtime
   b. Informal organization
   c. Organizational effectiveness
   d. Industrial relations

33. In the field of human resource management, _____ is the field concerned with organizational activity aimed at bettering the performance of individuals and groups in organizational settings. It has been known by several names, including employee development, human resource development, and learning and development.

Harrison observes that the name was endlessly debated by the Chartered Institute of Personnel and Development during its review of professional standards in 1999/2000.

   a. Revolving door syndrome
   b. Performance appraisal
   c. Person specification
   d. Training and development

34. _____ is an idea in the field of Organizational studies and management which describes the psychology, attitudes, experiences, beliefs and Values (personal and cultural values) of an organization. It has been defined as 'the specific collection of values and norms that are shared by people and groups in an organization and that control the way they interact with each other and with stakeholders outside the organization.'

This definition continues to explain organizational values also known as 'beliefs and ideas about what kinds of goals members of an organization should pursue and ideas about the appropriate kinds or standards of behavior organizational members should use to achieve these goals. From organizational values develop organizational norms, guidelines or expectations that prescribe appropriate kinds of behavior by employees in particular situations and control the behavior of organizational members towards one another.'

_____ is not the same as corporate culture.

Chapter 5. Functional strategies

a. Organizational development
b. Organizational culture
c. Organizational effectiveness
d. Union shop

35. _____ can be defined as the idea generation, concept development, testing and manufacturing or implementation of a physical object or service. _____ers conceptualize and evaluate ideas, making them tangible through products in a more systematic approach. The role of a _____er encompasses many characteristics of the marketing manager, product manager, industrial designer and design engineer.
   a. Abraham Harold Maslow
   b. Adam Smith
   c. Affiliation
   d. Product design

36. _____ is the use of control systems (such as numerical control, programmable logic control, and other industrial control systems), in concert with other applications of information technology (such as computer-aided technologies [CAD, CAM, CAx]), to control industrial machinery and processes, reducing the need for human intervention. In the scope of industrialization, _____ is a step beyond mechanization. Whereas mechanization provided human operators with machinery to assist them with the physical requirements of work, _____ greatly reduces the need for human sensory and mental requirements as well.
   a. AAAI
   b. A4e
   c. A Stake in the Outcome
   d. Automation

37. _____ refers to the overarching strategy of the diversified firm. Such a _____ answers the questions of 'in which businesses should we be in?' and 'how does being in these business create synergy and/or add to the competitive advantage of the corporation as a whole?'

Business strategy refers to the aggregated strategies of single business firm or a strategic business unit (SBU) in a diversified corporation. According to Michael Porter, a firm must formulate a business strategy that incorporates either cost leadership, differentiation or focus in order to achieve a sustainable competitive advantage and long-term success in its chosen arenas or industries.

   a. Strategic group
   b. Strategic drift
   c. Competitive heterogeneity
   d. Corporate Strategy

38. _____ are formal records of the financial activities of a business, person, or other entity. In British English, including United Kingdom company law, _____ are often referred to as accounts, although the term _____ is also used, particularly by accountants.

_____ provide an overview of a business or person's financial condition in both short and long term.

a. 1990 Clean Air Act
b. Financial statements
c. 28-hour day
d. 33 Strategies of War

39. In finance, a _____ or accounting ratio is a ratio of two selected numerical values taken from an enterprise's financial statements. There are many standard ratios used to try to evaluate the overall financial condition of a corporation or other organization. _____s may be used by managers within a firm, by current and potential shareholders (owners) of a firm, and by a firm's creditors.

a. Return on sales
b. Financial ratio
c. Return on equity
d. Rate of return

40. In finance, _____ refers to the way a corporation finances its assets through some combination of equity, debt, or hybrid securities. A firm's _____ is then the composition or 'structure' of its liabilities. For example, a firm that sells $20 billion in equity and $80 billion in debt is said to be 20% equity-financed and 80% debt-financed.

a. Capital budgeting
b. Shareholder value
c. Gross profit margin
d. Capital structure

41. _____ is an area of finance dealing with the financial decisions corporations make and the tools and analysis used to make these decisions. The primary goal of _____ is to maximize corporate value while managing the firm's financial risks. Although it is in principle different from managerial finance which studies the financial decisions of all firms, rather than corporations alone, the main concepts in the study of _____ are applicable to the financial problems of all kinds of firms.

a. Gross profit margin
b. Capital budgeting
c. Sweat equity
d. Corporate finance

Chapter 5. Functional strategies

42. _____ is the process of estimation in unknown situations. Prediction is a similar, but more general term. Both can refer to estimation of time series, cross-sectional or longitudinal data.
   a. Forecasting
   b. 1990 Clean Air Act
   c. 33 Strategies of War
   d. 28-hour day

43. The _____ of 2002 (Pub.L. 107-204, 116 Stat. 745, enacted July 30, 2002), also known as the Public Company Accounting Reform and Investor Protection Act of 2002 and commonly called Sarbanes-Oxley, Sarbox or SOX, is a United States federal law enacted on July 30, 2002, as a reaction to a number of major corporate and accounting scandals including those affecting Enron, Tyco International, Adelphia, Peregrine Systems and WorldCom.
   a. Sarbanes-Oxley Act
   b. Letter of credit
   c. Sarbanes-Oxley Act of 2002
   d. Fair Labor Standards Act

44. In economics, business, retail, and accounting, a _____ is the value of money that has been used up to produce something, and hence is not available for use anymore. In economics, a _____ is an alternative that is given up as a result of a decision. In business, the _____ may be one of acquisition, in which case the amount of money expended to acquire it is counted as _____.
   a. Cost
   b. Cost allocation
   c. Cost overrun
   d. Fixed costs

45. _____ , Total _____ , or Firm value (FV) is an economic measure reflecting the market value of the whole business. It is a sum of claims of all the security-holders: debtholders, preferred shareholders, minority shareholders, common equity holders, and others. _____ is one of the fundamental metrics used in business valuation, financial modeling, accounting, portfolio analysis, etc.
   a. AAAI
   b. A Stake in the Outcome
   c. A4e
   d. Enterprise value

Chapter 5. Functional strategies

46. _____ are defined as identifiable non-monetary assets that cannot be seen, touched or physically measured, which are created through time and/or effort and that are identifiable as a separate asset. There are two primary forms of intangibles - legal intangibles (such as trade secrets (e.g., customer lists), copyrights, patents, trademarks, and goodwill) and competitive intangibles (such as knowledge activities (know-how, knowledge), collaboration activities, leverage activities, and structural activities.) Legal intangibles are known under the generic term intellectual property and generate legal property rights defensible in a court of law.
   a. Interlocking directorate
   b. Induction programme
   c. Employee value proposition
   d. Intangible assets

47. In business and accounting, _____s are everything of value that is owned by a person or company. Any property or object of value that one possesses, usually considered as applicable to the payment of one's debts is considered an _____. Simplistically stated, _____s are things of value that can be readily converted into cash.
   a. Asset
   b. A Stake in the Outcome
   c. A4e
   d. AAAI

48. The _____ of 1996 (18 U.S.C. § 1831-1839) makes the theft or misappropriation of a trade secret a federal crime. Unlike Espionage, which is governed by Title 18 U.S. Code Sections 792 - 799, the offense involves commercial information, not classified or national defense information.
   a. AAAI
   b. Economic Espionage Act
   c. A Stake in the Outcome
   d. A4e

49. _____ is the process of understanding, anticipating and influencing consumer behavior in order to maximize revenue or profits from a fixed, perishable resource This process was first discovered by Dr. Matt H. Keller. The challenge is to sell the right resources to the right customer at the right time for the right price.
   a. Business networking
   b. Business model design
   c. Yield management
   d. Gap analysis

Chapter 6. Competitive strategies

1. _____ is, in very basic words, a position a firm occupies against its competitors.

According to Michael Porter, the three methods for creating a sustainable _____ are through:

1. Cost leadership

2. Differentiation

3. Focus (economics)

   a. Theory Z
   b. 1990 Clean Air Act
   c. 28-hour day
   d. Competitive advantage

2. Often a characteristic of new markets and industries, _____ occurs when technologies or offerings are so new that standards and rules are in flux, resulting in competitive advantages that cannot be sustained. In response, companies must constantly compete in price or quality, or innovate in supply chain management, new value creation, or have enough financial capital to outlast other competitors.
   a. Dominant Design
   b. NAIRU
   c. Learning-by-doing
   d. Hypercompetition

3. A _____ is a name or trademark connected with a product or producer. _____s have become increasingly important components of culture and the economy, now being described as 'cultural accessories and personal philosophies'.

Some people distinguish the psychological aspect of a _____ from the experiential aspect.

   a. Brand
   b. Brand awareness
   c. Brand loyalty
   d. Brand extension

4. _____, in marketing, consists of a consumer's commitment to repurchase or otherwise continue using the brand and can be demonstrated by repeated buying of a product or service or other positive behaviors such as word of mouth advocacy.

_____ is more than simple repurchasing, however. Customers may repurchase a brand due to situational constraints, a lack of viable alternatives, or out of convenience.

a. Brand extension
b. Brand image
c. Brand awareness
d. Brand loyalty

5. A niche market is the subset of the market on which a specific product is focusing on; Therefore the _____ defines the specific product features aimed at satisfying specific market needs, as well as the price range, production quality and the demographics that is intended to impact.

Every single product that is on sale can be defined by its niche market. As of special note, the products aimed at a wide demographics audience, with the resulting low price (due to Price elasticity of demand), are said to belong to the Mainstream niche, in practice referred only as Mainstream or of high demand.

a. Prevailing wage
b. Market niche
c. Labor intensive
d. Dominant logic

6. _____ is an integrated communications-based process through which individuals and communities discover that existing and newly-identified needs and wants may be satisfied by the products and services of others.

_____ is defined by the American _____ Association as the activity, set of institutions, and processes for creating, communicating, delivering, and exchanging offerings that have value for customers, clients, partners, and society at large. The term developed from the original meaning which referred literally to going to market, as in shopping, or going to a market to buy or sell goods or services.

a. Disruptive technology
b. Marketing
c. Market development
d. Customer relationship management

7. _____ can be defined as the idea generation, concept development, testing and manufacturing or implementation of a physical object or service. _____ers conceptualize and evaluate ideas, making them tangible through products in a more systematic approach. The role of a _____er encompasses many characteristics of the marketing manager, product manager, industrial designer and design engineer.

a. Adam Smith
b. Abraham Harold Maslow
c. Affiliation
d. Product design

8. A _____ is a set of exclusive rights granted by a state to an inventor or his assignee for a limited period of time in exchange for a disclosure of an invention.

The procedure for granting _____s, the requirements placed on the _____ee and the extent of the exclusive rights vary widely between countries according to national laws and international agreements. Typically, however, a _____ application must include one or more claims defining the invention which must be new, inventive, and useful or industrially applicable.

a. Labor Management Reporting and Disclosure Act
b. Federal Trade Commission Act
c. Food, Drug, and Cosmetic Act
d. Patent

Chapter 7. Corporate strategies

1. A _____ strategy targets non-buying customers in currently targeted segments. It also targets new customers in new segments. (Winer)

A marketing manager has to think about the following questions before implementing a _____ strategy: Is it profitable? Will it require the introduction of new or modified products? Is the customer and channel well enough researched and understood?

The marketing manager uses these four groups to give more focus to the market segment decision: existing customers, competitor customers, non-buying in current segments, new segments.

   a. Context analysis
   b. Product line
   c. Customer relationship management
   d. Market development

2. In business and engineering, new _____ is the term used to describe the complete process of bringing a new product or service to market. There are two parallel paths involved in the NProduct development process: one involves the idea generation, product design, and detail engineering; the other involves market research and marketing analysis. Companies typically see new _____ as the first stage in generating and commercializing new products within the overall strategic process of product life cycle management used to maintain or grow their market share.
   a. 28-hour day
   b. Product development
   c. 1990 Clean Air Act
   d. 33 Strategies of War

3. In microeconomics and management, the term _____ describes a style of management control. Vertically integrated companies are united through a hierarchy with a common owner. Usually each member of the hierarchy produces a different product or (market-specific) service, and the products combine to satisfy a common need.
   a. Vertical integration
   b. 33 Strategies of War
   c. 1990 Clean Air Act
   d. 28-hour day

4. In microeconomics and strategic management, the term _____ describes a type of ownership and control. It is a strategy used by a business or corporation that seeks to sell a type of product in numerous markets. _____ in marketing is much more common than vertical integration is in production.

Chapter 7. Corporate strategies

a. No-bid contract
b. Career development
c. Farmshoring
d. Horizontal integration

5. _____ is the term used to describe a situation where different entities cooperate advantageously for a final outcome. Simply defined, it means that the whole is greater than the sum of the individual parts. Although the whole will be greater than each individual part, this is not the concept of _____.

a. 33 Strategies of War
b. 28-hour day
c. 1990 Clean Air Act
d. Synergy

6. A _____ is a name or trademark connected with a product or producer. _____s have become increasingly important components of culture and the economy, now being described as 'cultural accessories and personal philosophies'.

Some people distinguish the psychological aspect of a _____ from the experiential aspect.

a. Brand extension
b. Brand awareness
c. Brand loyalty
d. Brand

7. _____ refers to the methods of practicing and using another person's business philosophy. The franchisor grants the independent operator the right to distribute its products, techniques, and trademarks for a percentage of gross monthly sales and a royalty fee. Various tangibles and intangibles such as national or international advertising, training, and other support services are commonly made available by the franchisor.

a. Franchising
b. 1990 Clean Air Act
c. ServiceMaster
d. 28-hour day

8. _____ is a term referring to any strategy, generally in business or politics, to increase the likelihood of negative results over positive ones for a party that attempts any kind of takeover. It derives from its original meaning of a literal _____ carried by various spies throughout history, taken when discovered to eliminate the possibility of being interrogated for the enemy's gain.

Chapter 7. Corporate strategies

In publicly held companies, various methods to avoid takeover bids are called '_____s'.

a. Poison pill
b. 28-hour day
c. 1990 Clean Air Act
d. 33 Strategies of War

9. The phrase mergers and _____s refers to the aspect of corporate strategy, corporate finance and management dealing with the buying, selling and combining of different companies that can aid, finance, or help a growing company in a given industry grow rapidly without having to create another business entity.

An _____, also known as a takeover or a buyout, is the buying of one company (the 'target') by another. An _____ may be friendly or hostile.

a. A4e
b. AAAI
c. Acquisition
d. A Stake in the Outcome

10. A _____ is an entity formed between two or more parties to undertake economic activity together. The parties agree to create a new entity by both contributing equity, and they then share in the revenues, expenses, and control of the enterprise. The venture can be for one specific project only, or a continuing business relationship such as the Fuji Xerox _____.

a. Civil Rights Act of 1991
b. Meritor Savings Bank v. Vinson
c. Patent
d. Joint venture

11. Procter is a surname, and may also refer to:

- Bryan Waller Procter (pseud. Barry Cornwall), English poet
- Goodwin Procter, American law firm
- _____, consumer products multinational

a. Procter ' Gamble
b. Downstream
c. Strict liability
d. Master and Servant Acts

12. An _____ is a person who has possession of an enterprise and assumes significant accountability for the inherent risks and the outcome. It is an ambitious leader who combines land, labor, and capital to create and market new goods or services. The term is a loanword from French and was first defined by the Irish economist Richard Cantillon.
   a. AAAI
   b. A Stake in the Outcome
   c. Entrepreneur
   d. A4e

13. In economics, business, retail, and accounting, a _____ is the value of money that has been used up to produce something, and hence is not available for use anymore. In economics, a _____ is an alternative that is given up as a result of a decision. In business, the _____ may be one of acquisition, in which case the amount of money expended to acquire it is counted as _____.
   a. Cost
   b. Cost overrun
   c. Cost allocation
   d. Fixed costs

14. In finance and economics, _____ or divestiture is the reduction of some kind of asset for either financial or ethical objectives or sale of an existing business by a firm. A _____ is the opposite of an investment.
   a. 33 Strategies of War
   b. 1990 Clean Air Act
   c. 28-hour day
   d. Divestment

15. _____ is the corporate management term for the act of reorganizing the legal, ownership, operational, or other structures of a company for the purpose of making it more profitable, or better organized for its present needs. Alternate reasons for _____ include a change of ownership or ownership structure, demerger repositioning debt _____ and financial _____.

Chapter 7. Corporate strategies

a. Net worth
b. Restructuring
c. Market value added
d. Market value

16. In law, _____ refers to the process by which a company (or part of a company) is brought to an end, and the assets and property of the company redistributed. _____ can also be referred to as winding-up or dissolution, although dissolution technically refers to the last stage of _____. The process of _____ also arises when customs, an authority or agency in a country responsible for collecting and safeguarding customs duties, determines the final computation or ascertainment of the duties or drawback accruing on an entry.

a. Liquidation
b. 33 Strategies of War
c. 1990 Clean Air Act
d. 28-hour day

17. _____ is a legally declared inability or impairment of ability of an individual or organization to pay its creditors. Creditors may file a _____ petition against a debtor ('involuntary _____') in an effort to recoup a portion of what they are owed or initiate a restructuring. In the majority of cases, however, _____ is initiated by the debtor (a 'voluntary _____' that is filed by the insolvent individual or organization.)

a. 28-hour day
b. 1990 Clean Air Act
c. Bankruptcy
d. 33 Strategies of War

18. The _____ is a chart that had been created by Bruce Henderson for the Boston Consulting Group in 1970 to help corporations with analyzing their business units or product lines. This helps the company allocate resources and is used as an analytical tool in brand marketing, product management, strategic management, and portfolio analysis. _____

To use the chart, analysts plot a scatter graph to rank the business units (or products) on the basis of their relative market shares and growth rates.

a. Marketing plan
b. Market segment
c. Marketing strategy
d. BCG matrix

Chapter 7. Corporate strategies

19. _____ is the process of comparing the cost, cycle time, productivity, or quality of a specific process or method to another that is widely considered to be an industry standard or best practice. Essentially, _____ provides a snapshot of the performance of your business and helps you understand where you are in relation to a particular standard. The result is often a business case for making changes in order to make improvements.

   a. Benchmarking
   b. Complementors
   c. Cost leadership
   d. Competitive heterogeneity

20. In business, a _____ is a product or a business unit that generates unusually high profit margins: so high that it is responsible for a large amount of a company's operating profit. This profit far exceeds the amount necessary to maintain the _____ business, and the excess is used by the business for other purposes.

   A firm is said to be acting as a _____ when its earnings per share (EPS) is equal to its dividends per share (DPS), or in other words, when a firm pays out 100% of its free cash flow (FCF) to its shareholders as dividends at the end of each accounting term.

   a. Workflow
   b. Middle management
   c. Design management in organization
   d. Cash cow

Chapter 8. Strategic management in other organization types

1. A _____ is a business that is privately owned and operated, with a small number of employees and relatively low volume of sales. The legal definition of 'small' often varies by country and industry, but is generally under 100 employees in the United States and under 50 employees in the European Union. In comparison, the definition of mid-sized business by the number of employees is generally under 500 in the U.S. and 250 for the European Union.
   a. Golden Boot Compensation
   b. Critical Success Factor
   c. Pre-determined overhead rate
   d. Small business

2. An _____ is a person who has possession of an enterprise and assumes significant accountability for the inherent risks and the outcome. It is an ambitious leader who combines land, labor, and capital to create and market new goods or services. The term is a loanword from French and was first defined by the Irish economist Richard Cantillon.
   a. A4e
   b. A Stake in the Outcome
   c. Entrepreneur
   d. AAAI

3. _____ is an organization's process of defining its strategy and making decisions on allocating its resources to pursue this strategy, including its capital and people. Various business analysis techniques can be used in _____, including SWOT analysis (Strengths, Weaknesses, Opportunities, and Threats) and PEST analysis (Political, Economic, Social, and Technological analysis) or STEER analysis involving Socio-cultural, Technological, Economic, Ecological, and Regulatory factors and EPISTEL (Environment, Political, Informatic, Social, Technological, Economic and Legal)

   _____ is the formal consideration of an organization's future course. All _____ deals with at least one of three key questions:

   1. 'What do we do?'
   2. 'For whom do we do it?'
   3. 'How do we excel?'

   In business _____, the third question is better phrased 'How can we beat or avoid competition?'. (Bradford and Duncan, page 1.)

   a. Strategic planning
   b. 33 Strategies of War
   c. 28-hour day
   d. 1990 Clean Air Act

4. The term '_____' refers to the concept of collecting information and attempting to spot a pattern in the information. In some fields of study, the term '_____' has more formally-defined meanings.

Chapter 8. Strategic management in other organization types 49

In project management _____ is a mathematical technique that uses historical results to predict future outcome.

a. Least squares
b. Regression analysis
c. Trend analysis
d. Stepwise regression

5. _____ or cause-related marketing refers to a type of marketing involving the cooperative efforts of a 'for profit' business and a non-profit organization for mutual benefit. The term is sometimes used more broadly and generally to refer to any type of marketing effort for social and other charitable causes, including in-house marketing efforts by non-profit organizations. _____ differs from corporate giving (philanthropy) as the latter generally involves a specific donation that is tax deductible, while _____ is a marketing relationship generally not based on a donation.

a. 1990 Clean Air Act
b. Relationship marketing
c. Cause marketing
d. 28-hour day

6. _____ is an integrated communications-based process through which individuals and communities discover that existing and newly-identified needs and wants may be satisfied by the products and services of others.

_____ is defined by the American _____ Association as the activity, set of institutions, and processes for creating, communicating, delivering, and exchanging offerings that have value for customers, clients, partners, and society at large. The term developed from the original meaning which referred literally to going to market, as in shopping, or going to a market to buy or sell goods or services.

a. Customer relationship management
b. Disruptive technology
c. Marketing
d. Market development

7. _____ is a broad label that refers to any individuals or households that use goods and services generated within the economy. The concept of a _____ is used in different contexts, so that the usage and significance of the term may vary.

Typically when business people and economists talk of _____s they are talking about person as _____, an aggregated commodity item with little individuality other than that expressed in the buy/not-buy decision.

a. Consumer
b. 28-hour day
c. 33 Strategies of War
d. 1990 Clean Air Act

ANSWER KEY

Chapter 1
1. c 2. c 3. d 4. d 5. a 6. d 7. d 8. b 9. a 10. d
11. b 12. d 13. d 14. d 15. c 16. d 17. a

Chapter 2
1. c 2. a 3. b 4. b 5. a 6. c 7. d 8. c 9. d 10. a
11. b 12. b 13. c 14. d 15. b

Chapter 3
1. b 2. a 3. d 4. c 5. b 6. b 7. c 8. b 9. d 10. d
11. d 12. d 13. a 14. d 15. c 16. d 17. a 18. d 19. d 20. c
21. c 22. d 23. c 24. b 25. c 26. d 27. a 28. b 29. c 30. d
31. a 32. c 33. b 34. c 35. a

Chapter 4
1. d 2. b 3. c 4. b 5. d 6. a 7. d

Chapter 5
1. b 2. b 3. d 4. d 5. d 6. c 7. a 8. c 9. d 10. b
11. b 12. d 13. d 14. d 15. b 16. d 17. d 18. c 19. b 20. d
21. c 22. d 23. b 24. a 25. c 26. b 27. d 28. d 29. d 30. d
31. d 32. d 33. d 34. b 35. d 36. d 37. d 38. b 39. b 40. d
41. d 42. a 43. a 44. a 45. d 46. d 47. a 48. b 49. c

Chapter 6
1. d 2. d 3. a 4. d 5. b 6. b 7. d 8. d

Chapter 7
1. d 2. b 3. a 4. d 5. d 6. d 7. a 8. a 9. c 10. d
11. a 12. c 13. a 14. d 15. b 16. a 17. c 18. d 19. a 20. d

Chapter 8
1. d 2. c 3. a 4. c 5. c 6. c 7. a

www.ingramcontent.com/pod-product-compliance
Lightning Source LLC
Chambersburg PA
CBHW081219230426
43666CB00015B/2811